HALO REPAIR

A Nudge Toward Wholeness

BOOKS BY BILL FIEST

According to Anonymous
(Words of wit, wisdom, humor, and guidance
by no one in particular)

70 x 7
(a peace that passeth all understanding
or forgiveness 101)

HALO REPAIR

A Nudge Toward Wholeness

Bill Fiest

Bill Fiest

B3 Publishing
A division of Dream Believer Factory, Inc.
Strongsville, Ohio

B3 Publishing
A Division of Dream Believer Factory, Inc
19428 Bennington Drive
Strongsville, OH 44136

Library of Congress Cataloging-in-Publication Data
        Fiest, Bill
                Halo Repair: a nudge toward wholeness /
                by Bill Fiest. – 1st ed.

                ISBN 0-9767849-0-4

Manufactured in the United States of America

For information regarding special discounts for bulk purchases
please contact the author at www.HaloRepair.com. or write to
B3 Publishing at the above address.

CONTENTS

The little things?
The little moments?
They aren't little.

- Jon Kabat-Zinn

FOREWORD

I believe we are all angels sent from Heaven to spread God's love and healing power. Our job is to minister to one another. What a marvelous calling – angels serving angels. Now why would one of God's angels need love and healing from another angel? Simple, sometimes we forget where we came from. That's where "Halo Repair" comes in. We need to be reminded of the source, of the healing love, and most of all, that it was this source of healing love that produced us. We are truly God's beloved, God's angels sent from heaven. Occasionally, we may need a little halo repair to be born again in the image and the likeness. We may need a nudge toward wholeness.

This is not an exhaustive work of every possible way of halo repair. And the instances put forth are not necessarily heroic, front-page headline sorts of stories. They're examples of everyday people living life. And from their lives come some illustrations of halo repair in action. Models you can use.

There will be stories, thoughts, quotes, and guidance for the reader to ponder for use in their own life. Just being aware that there's always halo repair to be done may help make each of us better able to minister to others and also better able to accept help in the repair and maintenance of our own halos.

That's my hope. Here's my effort.

Bill Fiest

Doing good to others
is not a duty.
It is a joy, for it increases your
own health and happiness.

- Zoroaster

I dedicate this book to my wife and son,
Debbie and Jason.
Their love and support have helped to keep my halo in
place for years.
I only hope I've done as much for theirs.
I love you both.

Believe in magic.

Live in wonder.

Dream in color.

- Old Greeting Card

DARLENE

I was walking on the sidewalk along Waikiki Beach one evening the first time I saw Darlene. She was obviously homeless, something I was surprised to see of in Hawaii. Of course, is there a better place to be homeless then in a tropical paradise? No cold winters of Cleveland, Ohio. I often wonder why there are homeless people in the North. If I was homeless, I believe I'd be working my way toward better year-round weather, since weather is where I always am.

Anyway, Darlene's feet were dirty and it looked like she had a badly infected cut on her big toe. Her clothing was dirty, she was filthy, and her body odor made you gasp.

I was haunted by Darlene's appearance and situation all the rest of that day and into a restless night. Here I was writing a book about halo repair and I was at a loss as to what to do for Darlene. (I named her Darlene sometime during the night when I awoke with her image on my mind.)

Finally, it dawned on me. I could do nothing. I did pray for her, but that was it. As angels we are expected to share the light when and where we can. But we can't do everything for everybody.

I'm reminded of a woman I worked with who was in a perpetual state of despair after seeing a story on TV about Romanian orphans. She couldn't shake the image of those sad faces and their hopeless situation. So much so that she was not able to have any joy in her life. Well, I'm here to tell you joy is important. As a matter of fact, I believe God is joy. God wants joy for all. It's a wonderful gift. We can do what we can, but we can't do what we can't. There will be times that the best we can do is direct love and healing through prayer and expect the best for those souls. So that's what we do. Then let it go and move on in our blessed roll as one of God's beloved. To spread joy and love we must be joy and love.

So, from my soul to Darlene's soul went the love of God. No follow up, just joyful expectation. It is an expectation that her soul's purpose will be fulfilled. That she'll touch others in a way that will enhance their lives. She had dramatically touched my life without even knowing it.

Now, this type of halo repair is something I do many times a day, whenever I hear an ambulance, see a frown, or read the paper. Halo repair doesn't have to be a physical action. It can be a loving, healing thought sent to another. Just that quick. Just that simple. A thought sent in knowing and joyful expectation that their soul is at ease in its purpose.

So I guess I *did* do something for Darlene. May God bless her soul.

One word
frees us of all the weight
and pain of life:
That word is love.

- Sophocles

Treat others as you would like to be treated.

- The Golden Rule

THE COMPANIONS

As I walked by Linda and Heather in the hallway at church, Heather asked if I was going to be part of "The Companions in Christ" class. I told her no, because I had already committed to 34 weeks of "Disciples" class on Monday evenings and I thought it would be too much to commit to 28 weeks of a class on Sunday morning. That's when Linda chimed in with the fact that she was doing both. I looked at them, realizing I was on the spot, and said I'd do it. It turned out to be one of the most life-enhancing classes in which I've ever participated.

The idea behind "Companions" is to build leaders through small group experiences. Over a period of 28 weeks, the group-building exercises would slowly mold a few followers into confident potential leaders. Now, when I say leaders, I'm not talking about up-in-the-pulpit preacher types. You could lead by example, chairing or serving on a committee, volunteering, supporting more vocal leaders, etc. Learning about working with others in a loving, affirming way makes being followed or following easier for everyone.

Although, I thoroughly enjoyed every class meeting, there was one in particular, and one person's response to our assignment, I will never forget. We were about 16 weeks into the class and becoming quite comfortable with each other. As we settled in with our coffee and muffins (Heather brought a different kind of homemade muffin each week), we prepared to go over our weekly homework assignments. One of the things we were to do was to rewrite a part of the Jesus' baptism scene but to have God's voice from heaven be talking to us. In other words, we would write as if God were talking to each of us, personally.

I really liked this assignment and thought I had done a pretty fair job. But I was blown away by the heartfelt responses of the other companions, especially Linda's.

Linda's interpretation of this part of the homework was so powerful that I asked if I could copy it after class. I then made refrigerator magnets of the verse for each of the companions. She had brought to life a God of such incredible love and joy and compassion that I instantly fell in love with Linda's God. I know I have believed in this God for a long time, but I had never enjoyed such a wonderful description.

So, I now present Linda's "And a voice came from Heaven." Please insert your name where indicated.

And a voice came from Heaven.
_____, I feel delight in you. We are
attached and I am devoted to you.
I will love you tenderly,
show you mercy,
be with you in your sorrow,
joys, and desires,
and give generously
of my blessings to you.

- Linda Donahue

Isn't that comforting? Isn't that beautiful? You cannot read this too often.   It is as powerful an example of halo repair as I've experienced. I hope it is as much for you.

The tendency of
man's nature to good
is like the tendency of water
to flow downwards.

- Mencius

Maybe you are here on earth to learn that life is what you make it, and it's to be enjoyed.

– Dick Stuphen

It's a funny thing about life;
if you refuse to accept
anything but the best,
you very often get it.

- Somerset Maugham

PRETTY LADY

In 1985 I was living in Cape May, a beautiful old resort town at the southern end of New Jersey. I was operating a gift shop in the lower level of a Victorian house. Naturally, I got to know the shop owners next to me. Susan was going through a divorce and was in total shock that it was happening. She never saw it coming. We talked often and I couldn't help doing what I could to help repair the self-esteem (halo) of this special angel. Being a poor, three-chord guitar player, and fancying myself a songwriter, I decided to write a song for Susan to cheer her up and give her hope.

When I finished "Pretty Lady" one evening, I called Susan and sang it to her over the phone. She cried. I cried. And the next day at the shop I got the biggest hug.

Ok – jump forward to 2002. I'm in the middle of the "Companions in Christ" 28-week class. We're on a weekend retreat at a picturesque United Methodist Church camp in the woods near Hiram, Ohio. By this time, I had grown close to several of the companions.

While walking the half-mile trek through the woods from the dining room back to the lodge, I heard a noise behind me. It was Heather. Heather was a young woman in our church who had been widowed after only a couple years and she was facilitating the "Companions" class. She and I had made a connection and had shared much over the past weeks – and even more on this retreat.

I waited for her to catch up with me and we continued the walk together. I had been contemplating singing "Pretty Lady" to her and figured now was as good a time as any. It's funny how opportunity presents itself when you decide to do something. So, in the woods on a cool early spring day, I sang my little two-minute ballad to Heather. When I was done, I said "That's it," we hugged, and continued toward the lodge.

One more jump in time – to one of the last classes of the Companions. As luck would have it, that Sunday I found myself in the class with Claire, Pat, Linda, & Heather – three divorced women and one widow. We had become very close over the past months and I felt "Pretty Lady" wanting to be sung again. So, for a third time, I sang my gift to those I cared for. And again, I felt I had made a good decision. Their tears brought tears to my eyes. My "Pretty Ladies" now numbered five.

For any others who could use a boost or some hope, I give you "Pretty Lady."

Pretty Lady

There's a Pretty Lady who is a friend of mine.
She is a blessing to the world, you know.
She's loving, brave, compassionate,
She's caring and she's kind,
Her smile sets her face aglow.

Her heart is full of love
Just waiting to be shared.
Befriend her and be tender.
Pretty Lady, is worth the care.

Sometimes Pretty Lady, she feels so all alone
And helpless not knowing what went wrong.
But the hands of time will heal her heart and home
And someone will sing the Pretty Lady's song.

Her heart is full of love
Just waiting to be shared.
Befriend her and be tender.
Pretty Lady, is worth the care.

I intended the song to reveal what I saw in these beautiful women and to announce it to the world. Helping others see the best in themselves makes their halo's shine for all to see. May God bless the world's "Pretty Ladies."

If your heart did not break now
and then…how would you
know it is there?

- Bette Bao Lord

In the midst of winter,
I finally learned that
there was in me
an invincible summer.

- Albert Camus

God gave burdens, also shoulders.

- Yiddish Proverb

A SIMPLE SMILE / A KIND WORD

All my life I have been aware of people that didn't seem to be enjoying life. It is something that is hard for me to understand because I absolutely love life. That's not to say that I have never been down or sad, but for the most part I have been a very happy person. And as I have grown in my relationship with God, I have become even happier.

Yeah, I count my blessings instead of sheep. I put on a happy face. I speak of happy memories at funerals and laugh. I have to say, I feel more like one of God's beloved children when I'm joyous then at any other time. So, whenever possible, I choose joy.

Many times I find myself in line to buy something and notice the cashier just going through the paces, obviously bored or unhappy. I always try to do or say something that will bring a smile to their face. Generally I say something that has to do with their appearance. It could be their hair, their eyes, their skin. Maybe their jewelry catches my eye. "What a beautiful necklace," I might say, or "You have the prettiest eyes." The goal is joy and happiness. I know I can live for weeks on a good, sincere compliment, so I'm assuming others can also.

Now, the age of chivalry may have passed, but I still open doors for people. I'll offer my arm to an elderly person nervously approaching a curb or steps. When doing so, I'm not sure if I'm helping repair their halo or mine. But it really doesn't matter. And it may not be halo repair so much as halo strengthening. A little preventative maintenance couldn't hurt.

So smile. It almost always comes back at you. Extend a helping hand. See the good in people and tell them about it. Be happy. Be joy. You'll be a walking, talking, living, breathing, mobile halo repair shop. Step right up! No waiting. Joy spoken here.

Regret looks back.

Worry looks ahead.

Joy looks around!

- Anonymous

What creates despair is the imagination, which insists on predicting millions of moments, thousands of days, and so drains you that you cannot live the moment at hand.

- Andre Dubus

Believe that life is worth living,
and your belief will help create
the fact.

- William James

CAROL'S PERFECTION

We were standing in a prayer circle, as we always do after choir, sharing our joys and concerns, and there was silence which, usually indicates that those who cared to verbalize were done and someone would soon wrap it all up with a short prayer. Then Carol spoke. I should have suspected something, because her husband Wil was at her side and he's usually with the tenors, since we just form a circle from where we are. "Wil and I got word from the doctor today," she said with her voice cracking. "I've been diagnosed with breast cancer." She continued, but my mind was racing. Wil was a widower whose first wife had died from breast cancer. How could this be happening? I heard mention of treatments, operation, more treatments, losing her hair. It all kind of blurred together. Tears were streaming down my face, which would usually cause me to look down. But I couldn't take my eyes off Carol.

Someone finally closed us with prayer and we all took our turns hugging Carol. I don't remember what I said when I hugged Carol but I do remember imagining every ounce of healing love in my body being transferred to her. It's all I had to offer at the time but I was determined to do more.

I had attended several weekend seminars on directed prayer over the last several years, with Debbie, my wife. The idea is to focus on a specific situation and direct the healing, loving light of God toward its perfection. I truly believed in the process, but lacked the discipline to use it on a regular basis. That was about to change.

When I awoke, at noon, and when I went to bed, I pictured Carol's perfection. When she announced that her white blood cells or red blood cells needed to be at a certain count, I went to work. I saw her

21

being tested and getting the necessary positive results. All the while, I saw her perfect. No lump. No cancer. It may be done unto you as you believe, but sometimes it's your belief that needs help. And I wanted my belief to strengthen Carol's.

Now Carol had many people praying for her and loving her. So my contributions to her wellness may be neither here nor there. But I couldn't see her anyway but perfect. And I told her so every chance I got. I hugged her often and I'm sure I don't have to tell you about the value of a loving hug. When I prayed for the lump and cancer to go away, I couldn't picture it going. As far as I could tell there wasn't anything wrong with Carol. That's why I kept telling her she was perfect.

Carol went through the recommended treatments and the lump disappeared. Her beautiful red hair grew back even more beautiful. Carol's cancer brought to me a gift I had been promising myself for years: the gift of disciplined *daily* meditation and prayer. It's as valuable a gift as you can give yourself. I only wish that it hadn't taken a friend's cancer for me to get it. Whatever works, I guess. Now my halo is in better shape and Carol is too.

Today is a new day.
You will get out of it just what
you put into it.

– Mary Pickford

Sometimes
I sits and thinks,
and sometimes
I just sits.

- Satchel Paige

SELF-RESTORATION

"NO LIFEGAURD ON DUTY," read the sign next to my chair at the pool. Some people go through life that way. Like they are on their own and the world is conspiring against them. There's no one there to keep them from drowning. Just their luck!

Well, life is that way if that's what you believe. "It's done unto you as you believe" is not a bumper sticker. It's the real thing. You need to remind yourself whose you are. You are God's beloved child. As was mentioned many times in Neale Donald Walsch's "Conversations with God" books, "re-minding" yourself literally means changing your mind.

God's angels are not conspiring against you. They are conspiring for you. They want to do you good. Believe it! Watch for it! Expect it!

In James Allen's classic, "As A Man Thinketh," he speaks of a person's mind as a garden. Left untended, anything that lands in it can grow. He says to tend your mind's garden diligently. Put the destructive weeds out and only allow in the loving, joyful, healing seeds that can be nourished into a beautiful life.

That's how self-restoration works. It starts inside each of us and grows as nourished. What is wonderful about it is that we don't always have to do all the work ourselves. Just recognizing yourself as one of God's angels opens you to other angels as they come into your life.

HALO REPAIR

Your halo can be repaired whether you believe you have a halo or not. Believing is the self-restorative act that hastens the process. I would think choosing a joyful journey through life would be preferable. But that's just me. You can do what you want. So be careful, because you really do become what you think about most of the time. Be your own lifeguard. Mind your own mind. It's a garden (and halo) worth tending.

We must cultivate
our garden.

- Voltaire

You have no idea
what a poor opinion
I have of myself–
and how little I deserve it.

- W.S. Gilbert

UNCONDITIONAL LOVE

I don't remember the occasion, but I remember vividly what I said. It was when my son Jason was seven or eight years old and I looked him right in the eye and told him, "I will always love you. No matter what! Even if you killed your mother I would still love you. I would come and visit you in prison because that's where you should be, but I will always love you."

I wanted him to know my love is unconditional. Always there, even if I'm angry or upset. Nothing can affect my love for him. I think this is very important, not only for children but for others we love, also.

When I was 35, I remember deciding to tell my mom I love her every time I talked to her. Now this may sound like no big deal to some people, but I wasn't raised in a demonstrative family. We didn't do stuff like that. It was very hard, at first, but now it's a wonderful habit. And, of course, I do the same thing with my wife Debbie and my son Jason.

Now, I said that this was a decision and it was. This was a conscious effort on my part not to put my candle under a bushel. It serves better when shared. And having my mom, my wife, and my son say it back to me brings a spit shine to my halo I couldn't achieve alone.

So let the light of your love shine unabashedly. It doesn't serve anyone to play small with the gifts God has given you. Share your halo-repairing self with the world and stand back and enjoy the blinding glow of halos all around you.

For a long time it seemed to me that life
was about to begin–real life.
But there was always some obstacle in
the way.
Something to be gotten through first,
some unfinished business, time still to be
served, a debt to be paid.
At last it dawned on me that these
obstacles *were* my life.
This perspective has helped me to see
there is no way to happiness.
Happiness is the way.
So treasure every moment you have and
remember that time waits for no one.

Happiness is a journey, not a destination.

\- Souz

If you ever find happiness by
hunting for it, you will find it,
as the old woman did her lost
spectacles, on her nose
all the time.

- Josh Billings

Whatever you can do, or dream
you can, begin it.
Boldness has genius, power,
and magic in it.

– Goethe

JODI'S STORY

My favorite and the most beautiful story of self-inflicted halo repair I know is about Jodi. Jodi and I are members of the NEWSingers choir at our church. The NEWSingers choir is such a wonderful, caring, loving, and supportive church family that it's almost painful to miss a practice. Their halo-restorative powers are so great that you might leave with two halos.

Jodi works in the social services field, which is not the happiest of arenas. She's also had her own bouts with depression. When she gets home at the end of a work day, she's often drained. And even though she knows full well that going to choir practice and being in that room full of angels would be good for her, she often can't seem to drag herself from the couch to the door of her apartment.

So what does Jodi do? She has enlisted a fellow choir member to pick her up and take her to choir. Because with someone else being involved, she knows she has to get ready on time. And when asking for help, she said she needed to be pushed and not to let her off the hook easily. What a brave, bold move to get herself where she knows she needs to be.

Jodi's story is so inspiring to me because I don't ask for help. And God knows I should. Oh, I'll ask God for help, but I'm not that keen on asking God's earthly angels to help me personally. I love helping others and I love hugs and compliments and more hugs. But to do what Jodi did has not been part of my being. I'm fine. How can I help you?

Jodi's courage and example in taking care of herself has humbled me. She knew what she needed and made arrangements to cause it to happen, even if it meant asking for help.

I have vowed never again to shirk my repair responsibility for my own halo. If I can't do it, I surely know someone willing to drive me to the repair shop. And now, because of one of God's beloved angels, I'm not too proud to ask.

Thank you, Jodi.

What a wonderful
life I've had!
I only wish I'd
realized it sooner.

- Colette

Don't discount the importance
of being around people who
love you.

– Bill Fiest

MY ONE LEGGED HUNGARIAN

The summer of 2000 was one for the books. For over five years, my wife Debbie had been helping take care of her father who was suffering from post-polio syndrome. We got a call one night in July that he had fallen out of bed and hit his head on the dresser. After three days in the hospital, he was sent to rehab at a nursing home near the hospital. A place he never left.

July was also the month my family was hosting a huge family reunion. Needless to say, I was very busy with that, though Debbie would help as much as she could.

In August, Debbie's mother had major surgery, which she should have had much earlier. Her mother kept putting it off because she was taking care of her husband. With him in the nursing home, she could now pay attention to herself.

Now it was Debbie's turn to be attended to. In June, an open sore had begun to develop on her "bad" leg. Debbie lost the use of her right leg when she was seven years old because of bone cancer. The subsequent radiation and heat treatments had left her leg barely usable and, eventually, she ended up using crutches full time. But the main thing was that the bone cancer was gone. She had beat it. Then, 40 years later, in the midst of taking care of her parents and preparing for a family reunion, she was in a lot of pain. Was this the cancer returning? My pleas to see a doctor were met with "after Mom's surgery I'll go, I promise."

Debbie is a dedicated daughter and a wonderful wife. Her selflessness was to be admired, but now I felt it was going too far. I was up against her Hungarian stubbornness. It was very hard watching the woman I love suffer. July and August were the longest two months of our life. Neither of us said anything, but the return of cancer was on our minds.

When I first met Debbie one of the things that I noticed about her was the way she carried herself. I had never seen a person on crutches with such perfect posture. Cute, self-confident–I just had to ask her out. Less than six months later we were married. Then here we were, 11 years later, and Debbie knew she was, at least, going to lose her leg. At worst, the cancer was back. We went to the doctor to have the sore looked at. We were called later that same day and told to be at the Cleveland Clinic the first thing in the morning. That made for a very scary night.

Dr. Joyce explained that this was a radiation eruption and would not heal. The leg would have to be removed immediately. I asked if the cancer had returned and he said no. He then said we'd have to make a decision right away and gave us time to ourselves to deal with the situation.

When Dr. Joyce left the room we looked at each other, hugged, and started crying and laughing at the same time. The leg might be coming off, but it wasn't cancer. Right away Debbie was talking about walking without crutches for the first time in years. She would be getting a prosthesis. It was kind of exciting. And that's the way she looked at it. As a blessing that would make her life better.

What an attitude to carry into surgery. All around her people were amazed at how she was able to joke around about having her leg amputated. That's when I started calling her my one-legged Hungarian.

She now has a prosthesis and walks without crutches. And she talks, too. While visiting her dad in the nursing home, she encouraged a woman who had lost her leg to diabetes. "Life isn't over," she said, "it's just different. Nothing you can't handle. Look at me. **I can dance with my husband."**

And she works out at the gym. I can't tell you how many people she's inspired there. By golly, if she's doing all this with one leg, who am I not to be taking care of myself when I have two good legs.

Her attitude and unembarrassed willingness to talk about her amputation has made my one-legged Hungarian honey, a halo-repairer of an inspirational magnitude.

There are shortcuts to
happiness
and dancing is one of them.

- Vicki Baum

The trick is in what one
emphasizes. We either make
ourselves miserable, or we
make ourselves happy.
The amount of work
is the same.

- Carlos Castaneda

I am an old man and have known a great many troubles, but most of them never happened.

- Mark Twain

OSTRACIZED

The other day I had lunch with a business associate who used to be Amish. I asked him if there were any repercussions with his family for leaving the Amish tradition. He said that he has no contact with his family, by their choice. He will not be permitted to even attend his parents' or sibling's funerals when they die. He's been told that by leaving he has assured his place in hell. A Mennonite friend of his counseled him that he would not be going to hell for that reason but he'll be going to hell because he wasn't saved. The fear and agony this good Christian has suffered on behalf of family and friends has been overwhelming at times. He has been hospitalized for depression. He worries about his children and their eternal souls. Just listening to him and seeing his body slumped as he spoke made me wonder, "Where's the love?"

I asked him if he believed in a loving God. Did he believe that God's love was the greatest love of all? "Absolutely," was his answer. I then asked him if he would say or do such things to his children as were done to him. "Absolutely NOT," he said. I told him that I believed that God loved him and his family more than he could ever understand. And, just as he wouldn't condemn his children to eternal suffering, that God would do no such thing to him. God loved him and he should always remember that.

Now, I don't know if this young man will ever be able to repair the rift in his family. It's probably too deep and ingrained. But I do know that God loves him and his family. And I told him so. He seemed to straighten up and, I believe, drew a breath of relief. We finished our lunch and he mentioned that he'd like to get together again. I said I'd love to.

HALO REPAIR

Halo repair means always being on the lookout for these precious opportunities to pass on your love and God's love. (I believe they are one and the same.) May we always be on the lookout for occasions to be good and pleasant and help others live together in unity, whether or not others are willing.

Visitor: "Henry, have you made your peace with God?"

Thoreau: "We have never quarreled."

God is a verb.

- Buckminster Fuller

GOD BLESS YOU, JASON FIEST

Many thoughts were going through my mind as my son Jason was getting ready to leave for the University of Toledo. Was he ready? Was I ready? Have I taught him everything he needs to know? Does he remember everything I tried to teach him? I really tried to give him more and more independence as he grew up. I figured the more the better since I would be nearby to help him when he needed it. He was going to be over two hours away with no adult supervision. I say that fully realizing that Jason is now an adult and would be supervising himself. Yikes!

My mind was filled with terror and excitement, loathing and joy, letting go and holding on. Jason had become a young man and I would soon know the full extent of his character as he presented himself to the world.

So, as a last ditch effort to put in my two cents, I composed a letter and stuck it in a book that we had bought for him about going to college. Here's the letter.

GOD BLESS YOU, JASON FIEST

You have no idea how proud I am of you, watching you grow over these eighteen years into such a wonderful young man. You've never been a disappointment to me. I can honestly say that you have turned out much better than I had ever planned. And there are so many people to thank for their input. Good and bad. Jason, you seemed to have acquired a very good sensibility about you. What an extraordinary gift for a person of your age. It will serve you well the rest of your life.

With such a gift, you'll be able to enjoy college to the fullest. The many different people and events you'll encounter will be awesome. Your growth will be your own. I have no doubt that college will be more delightful than not.

You have a solid base of faith and love that will sustain you. God has blessed you, Jason, and I have been so honored and blessed to have been you father. Thanks for making it an easy job.

All my love,
Dad

I don't know if the letter was for him or me. But I sure felt a lot better after writing it. And, about a week after he got to school, I got a phone call saying that he had just found the letter and loved it. Tears still well up in my eyes when I think of that call. Fortunately, tears are wonderful for polishing up halos.

There is no greater joy in life
than a child going
down the road singing
after asking me the way.

- Anonymous

The greatest gifts my parents gave to me…were their unconditional love and a set of values. Values that they lived and didn't just lecture about.

- Colin Powell

THE GRANDMA BOOK

As Mother's Day approached a few years ago, I was trying to think of something special for my mom. I finally came up with the idea of "The Grandma Book." I would have each of the thirteen grandchildren and four great-grandchildren do a page for Grandma's book. And they could do anything they wanted.

Some wrote notes with crayon drawings. Some did a picture collage of themselves. Still others put in poems or wrote letters of love and appreciation. One even wrote an apology for something he had done years before. The little ones had their hands stamped on the page with "I love you, Grandma" written by their moms. And, of course, there were stickers throughout.

I made up a cover that said "I Love My Grandma" in a children's script font I had found on my computer. I then took these 17 pages of pure love and mixed them up and had them plastic comb bound.

We all got together for Mother's Day and presented it to her. Her eyes were watery from page one right through the end. Mom still has this book on display in her living room for all to see. It was so much fun to see her halo get so much attention from the ones' whose halos she had tended and mended their entire lives. And she's still tending halos everywhere she goes. I love you, Mom!

My religion
is very simple–
my religion
is kindness.

- Dalai Lama

The world is a great mirror.
It reflects back what you are.

- Thomas Dreier

Mae West: For a long time I was ashamed of the way I lived.

Reporter: Did you reform?

Mae West: No; I'm not ashamed anymore.

ANNIVERSARY CARDS

Last week was our anniversary. We got married on Debbie's birthday, so if I forget one, I forget both. Double trouble. And it has happened, but not this year. After we exchanged cards, we hugged and kissed. I was about to put my card on the bookshelf in my den when a thought occurred to me. These cards express lovely thoughts that are very true but rarely expressed to each other. I thought, "What if, after reading the cards, we returned them to each other. Then every morning when we awoke we could read this wonderful sentiment we felt about our spouses and then read them again before we saw them at the end of the work day."

How would this affect our relationship, to be reminded of our true loving feelings in the tender moments when the tender moments aren't necessarily happening? Would these words of overwhelming love come in handy any other times? I'll bet they could. It's often not convenient to remember how much or why you love someone. You really don't want to, especially when they don't live up to your expectations.

So, instead of throwing away those old anniversary cards, you might want to put aside a couple of the good ones in a place that they're readily available. Look at them when you're sulking. Read them when you're angry. Hold them when you don't feel like holding anything. Remember, faults are thick where love is thin! Don't let your love get thin. Work on your lover's halo and you'll be working on yours, too.

To my husband–
I love you more
than words can say.

- Hallmark Greeting Card

Keep your old love letters.
Throw away your old bank
statements.

– Mary Schmich

Can there be a love which does
not make demands on its
object?

- Confucius

HUGS–EMBRACING REPAIR

There's a gentleman at the United Methodist Church of Berea named Robbie. Robbie is known for a number of wonderful things but I believe that the one he's most known for is giving out hugs. He even has a button that reads "FREE HUGS".

I think this man has nourished more halos with his hug vitamins than anyone could count. When you see him on Sunday morning, or at any other church event, you often see him locked in an embrace. And these are real hugs. Not those little courtesy touches you see some people do. I really don't know how he does it. He's certainly in great hugging shape.

One year, during the Christmas season, the NEWSingers choir decided that Robbie's house would be one of our stops when we went caroling. I rode in Linda's van with several others. When we finished caroling for Robbie, we all hustled back to our respective vehicles. Those of us in Linda's van were waiting in the cold winter night for Linda to come and unlock the doors. After a few minutes, which seemed like longer, Linda arrived and I asked her, in my best shivering and irritated voice, what took her so long. She said she was stuck in a hug.

STUCK IN A HUG! And it was with the master of hugs. Does it get any better than that? The look on her face was joy. When you're stuck in a hug, other people waiting an extra few minutes really doesn't matter that much.

Hugging is a wonderful way to share yourself. When you hug someone, from the heart, there is a melding of spirit that can lift and strengthen just about anyone. And it doesn't deplete your spirit by doing so. God has made sure there is a never-ending supply of the God-Spirit to share and pass around.

Personally, I've always been able to hug the women. Hugging men has been the challenge for me. But now that I understand the value of a sincere hug I share it with all. God's love knows no boundaries, so I guess hugs shouldn't either.

So form a halo with your arms and embrace someone's spirit. Getting stuck in a hug may be the high point of their day–and yours.

There is not enough darkness
in the world
to extinguish the light
of one small candle.

- Spanish proverb

I am an optimist.
It does not seem
too much sense
being anything else.

- Sir Winston Churchill

FORGIVENESS–
THE SILENT HEALER

I really don't want to do this story. I'm not proud of myself for some of the hatred and ill will I've harbored for years. There have been things that have happened in my life that I've felt I could never forgive. I've been so hurt and angered that I've prayed for people to die. For nearly a year I did that. Not good.

I've taken courses on forgiveness. I've read books and listened to tapes. I just couldn't see how any of it could be possible. But somewhere deep inside me I knew something needed to be done. So I finally decided to try some of the things I had learned about forgiveness.

The simplest of these was to sit and mentally forgive everyone I needed to forgive, and to forgive my self. It sounded silly, and I expected nothing to come of it, but of all the suggestions, it was the easiest. And heaven knows I didn't want to work at this.

Simply saying, "I forgive so and so for whatever," or "I forgive myself for whatever," is more powerful than you might imagine. It may take several sittings and you might not believe what you're doing, but forge ahead anyway. Keep it simple with no conditions. Forgive and forget.

Peter McWilliams, in his book "You Can't Afford The Luxury Of A Negative Thought," suggests you wait five years before judging anything. Wait five years before you decide if you've been wronged. He says if you don't think you can remember it for five years, then good, forget it now.

Of course, some of us can do five years standing on our head. I can and I have. But no more. It's simply not worth it. I would never have believed this if I hadn't finally made myself try it. You may have to forgive over and over again. Don't be discouraged. It may take as many times as you've remembered the perceived wrong. (OK, it was more than perceived, but now's the time to let it go.)

Teach yourself to forgive instantly. It'll save a lot of wear and tear on your mind and body, and you're not getting any younger. Make it a habit and you may be surprised how quick an upset can go away. And always forgive yourself no matter what. You are a blessed child of God and you are forgiven and ready to move on. Live and learn. Love. Be joyful. Let it go! A halo is for wearing, not for beating yourself over the head with.

I no longer pray for a certain person's death. I have forgiven them and myself for the incident. I want to be happy and hating makes that tough. I've let go and moved on in joy. I feel free and I love it.

Forgiveness may be the most important act in halo repair there is. Don't take it lightly. Loving yourself and others requires it.

To be wronged is nothing
unless you continue
to remember it.

- Confucius

Always
forgive your enemies–
nothing annoys
them so much.

- Oscar Wilde

YOU COULD GET HIT BY A BUS

We got off the trolley bus about three blocks from our hotel. I was carrying a shopping bag in each hand and so I was not holding Debbie's hand, as usual, as we began walking. Within a few steps an event was set in motion that still brings me chills and goose bumps.

My wife Debbie is an above the knee amputee. She does quite well walking with her prosthesis but really has to watch so that she doesn't trip because it's hard for her to catch her balance.

As we began our trek to the hotel, Debbie tripped over an uneven spot in the sidewalk and she started falling towards the street. She got to the curb just as a city bus was going by. With her hands out in front of her she hit the side of the bus just behind the front doors. This spun her around and she fell down on the curb and rolled under the bus.

I had dropped the bags and was right behind her as she fell. I can remember reaching under the bus to pull her out and thinking "Oh, my God, the tires!" Her legs and body were lined up with the dual rear wheels of the bus. Debbie said she heard me scream, "Oh, my God, the tires!" So apparently I didn't just think it. I rolled Debbie up against the curb just as the rear wheels whizzed by. I swear I could have stuck out my tongue and touched the bus, it was that close.

How I had time to pull my wife out from under a moving bus was answered after the bus stopped and the bus driver was coming back to us. A passenger on the bus had hollered to the driver to stop because somebody fell under the bus. Immediately, the driver hit the brakes to slow the bus down and stop it. Thank God for that passenger and the quick acting driver, as I just barely had time to roll her out of the way.

The poor bus driver got off the bus to see the two of us lying next to the curb. He thought he had run over someone. After a few minutes of listening to the accounts of the driver, passenger, and passersby we were able to reconstruct the incident. Debbie was skinned up a little bit, but none the worse considering what had just happened. We sent the driver on his way, calmed down a hysterical woman on a park bench, and hobbled back to the hotel.

The following week was amazing. The incident was just a blur to Deb and she had never really felt the danger. For me, on the other hand, it was a nightmare. I realized that if I hadn't rolled her out from under that bus I would have been right next to her as those dual rear wheels ran over the length of her body. It was a thought that haunted me for over a week. So much so, that I had a hard time sleeping without seeing the bus and Deb under it.

I'm better now. But I still get chills when I tell the story. We've even added a little humor to the account. I didn't know where I had grabbed Debbie when I rolled her out, but I knew she bruised easily and the next day we would see the marks I left. We were so right. She had a black-and-blue mark the shape of my hand on her right buttock. It was actually a comic relief for us. And I, for one, really needed a reason to laugh.

I tell this story because I believe it is a wonderful example of the world conspiring for us. There was a chorus of angels that all sang their notes at precisely the right time, and all without rehearsal. The passenger on the bus, the driver, and I worked together to make sure this delightful angel of mine would be wearing her halo for many years to come.

Of course, you might ask why Debbie had to trip if the world is conspiring for us. My answer to that is "why not?" Tripping is just part of life. I wouldn't expect the laws of the universe to be suspended just for us. We live life and take it as it comes, not always understanding, but always trying to pull the best from it.

Deb knew how shook up I was from this and it reaffirmed our love at a time when she had lost one of the people that loved her. Her mother had died recently and, despite my best efforts, she was feeling alone. Well, having your husband pull you out from under a moving bus can heal a multitude of wounds. So it was with us. She now knows there is plenty of love for her–right here, right now. A love that heals, a love that gives hope, a love that embraces, a love that listens, and a love that endures.

It can be amazing what it takes to repair or restore a halo. Sometimes it takes being hit by a bus—almost.

My advice to you is not to
inquire why or whither,
but just enjoy the ice cream
while it's on your plate.

– Thornton Wilder

I don't want to get to the end of
my life and find that I just lived
the length of it.
I want to have lived the width
of it as well.

– Diane Ackerman

The New England conscience doesn't stop you from doing what you shouldn't; it just keeps you from enjoying it.

- Cleveland Amory

ANONYMOUS REPAIR

Each year my church sets up a giving tree at Christmas time. On it are tags with gift wishes from people in the community that have fallen on hard times. The tag may say "boys underwear," with the size wanted and the age of the boy. It might be gloves for a 55-year-old man or a robe for a 32-year-old woman. My wife Debbie and I are always humbled by the requests, since our own lists for Christmas are much different from underwear and gloves. When you take a tag you are responsible for buying that item, wrapping it, and returning it to the church before Christmas.

We have such a good time with this project, especially Debbie. She wraps the gifts beautifully and is always able to think of some extra little thing to put in with the requested item. One year a ten-year-old boy wanted a box that locks. Now, trying to get into the mind of a ten-year-old boy to figure out why he would want a box that locks can be challenging. We figured he needed a place to keep his private stuff, like things he found and what not. Imagine his surprise when he not only got the box, but inside were a bag of M&M's and ten dollars. With the robe for the woman, Debbie had put bath salts and body oil. Debbie is so thoughtful.

These gifts were given anonymously, so one could only envision the recipient opening them on Christmas. And what a vision that is. We've both experienced joyful receiving enough to be able to picture the faces. Here are people getting presents from strangers. We can only imagine their joy and appreciation. Who says there isn't a Santa Claus? If they enjoy receiving as much as we enjoy giving then I would think their halos were a few shades brighter that day. I know ours were brightened up earlier as we shopped, wrapped, and dropped off the gifts at the church.

HALO REPAIR

This is only one small example of the anonymous repair of halos. I'm sure you can think of many others on your own. Sometimes it's a spur of the moment thing and other times it's well thought out. It's giving without giving a thought to receiving thanks. It's being good for goodness sake. You'll feel better if you watch out for opportunities to commit an unthanked act of kindness. Knowing you've improved another's halo is thanks enough. And I'm sure your halo is none the worse for the effort.

The greatest pleasure I know
is to do a good action by
stealth,
and to have it found out by
accident.

- Charles Lamb

We may give without loving,
but we cannot love
without giving.

- Anonymous

ROAD RAGE AND
THE ROCKFORD FILES

Screeching tires made me look up as I was going to my car. A man in a pickup had sped around in front of a man in a car and slammed on the brakes. He jumped out of the truck and stomped towards the car screaming. The man in the car got out, but stood with the open car door between them. I took a step to go back to the office and call the police when the pickup truck driver ran to his vehicle and took out an ax handle. I knew something had to be done right now.

You see, the previous evening I had watch James Garner in the "Rockford Files." In this episode, he stopped a guy from hitting a woman. I mentioned to my wife how much courage it would take to insert yourself in a situation like that and I admired Rockford for doing it. I know it's just a TV show, but I was impressed nonetheless.

Now, the man from the pickup was spitting on the car, cursing, and waving an ax handle around. The driver of the car was saying nothing. As the ax handle was raised I heard myself saying, "Hey! What's going on here?" And I started walking towards the men. As I arrived between them, the pickup driver was yelling that the car had cut him off back down the street and endangered him and his children. I said, "You have children in the truck? Don't you think they're upset watching their father threatening a man with an ax handle?"

He screamed, "Well, he has a knife!" My heart sank. Here I am between a guy with an ax handle and a guy with a knife. I turned to the driver of the car and asked him if he had a knife. He showed me a folding hunter with a four-inch blade. I looked him right in the eye and told him to put it away. He did. I drew a breath and turned and told the other guy to put down the club. He did. I was amazed. Jim Rockford had nothing on me.

I then listened as the truck driver yelled his story to me. This seemed to calm him down a bit, so I said that he should take the license number of the car and make a report, if he's that upset and concerned. Also, he should get back in his pickup truck, calm down, and leave with his children. He did just that. I turned to the guy in the car and asked him if he was all right. He answered he was and I told him to have a nice day as I turned and left.

When I told my wife what had happened that day, she was furious. What did I think I was doing getting between guys with knives and clubs? Maybe it was the "Rockford Files" or maybe I'm just stupid but I couldn't walk away. I was afraid that someone was going to get very badly hurt or killed and I did what I felt was needed.

I don't recommend doing what I did. I haven't done it since. Of course, the opportunity hasn't arisen. If I had felt personally threatened, which I didn't, I probably would have gone back into the office and phoned the police. But I had to at least distract them by asking what's going on. Sometimes all people need is to have their attention diverted to completely change the situation.

The drivers may not have left the scene feeling any different about one another, but they did leave without their halos being bashed in. For that we thank Jim Rockford.

What lies before us
and what lies behind us
are tiny matters
compared to what
lies within us.

- Ralph Waldo Emerson

One person can
and does
make a difference.

- Albert Schweitzer

WHERE SELDOM IS HEARD AN ENCOURAGING WORD

Mike and Suzie adopted a brother and sister from Russia. They were a couple of beautiful children for a wonderful couple. Mike and Suzie have been such loving parents to these kids and you can see it in their interaction when you're around them. The kids are well behaved but still fun-loving children. Mike and Suzie enjoy being parents and are doing a superb job of it.

Deb and I were at their house one day and I was commenting on what a great job they're doing as parents. Mike was thankful, but said that they have friends who told them to take pleasure in the early years, because when the kids become teenagers they will hate your guts.

I was stunned. Why would you tell someone something like that? Was that their experience as parents and that made it the universal truth?

I told Mike not to worry. If you're a loving father and husband it will rub off on the kids. They'll see how you treat them and their mother with love and respect, then it will be innate in them as they grow up and they'll return that love and respect to you. That's been my experience and I'm sure it'll be yours.

He said he hoped I was right, because it really worries him to think of his kids turning against him and his wife.

On the way home, I told Deb about the conversation I had had with Mike. Neither of us could imagine why someone would want to discourage parents. Why plant that seed of doubt and make them think it's all for naught? That no matter what they do now it could all fall apart when the kids become teenagers.

I grant you that the teenage years can be challenging, but that doesn't mean every minute of every day. It's a time when kids are testing their independence and parents are walking the fine line of how much freedom they can handle. And when I say "they" I mean the parents, mostly.

If you tend to your children's halos, as they grow they'll be better able to tend to their own. Learning that ability isn't bad and it doesn't mean they don't need or love you anymore. It just means they're growing up. And they'll remember where to come when they need a little halo restoration, because Mom and Dad have shown they are experts in the field. They are their children's personal trainers when it comes to halo repair. And it should be taken seriously.

Keeping this in mind as they grow will also be good for your own halo. The joy you'll get from their successes and growth will be reflected from your halo for all to see. Even those who told you your children would eventually hate your guts.

Mike and Suzie are dedicated, loving parents and their kids will always know that and mirror that. Their halos will live on.

All children behave
as well as they
are treated.

- Anonymous

You don't really understand
human nature unless you know
why a child on a
merry-go-round will wave at
his parents every time around–
and why his parents will
always wave back

    – William D. Tammeus

ACT TWO: THE NIGHTMARE

I got a call from Carol. She said, "I need for you to pray for me. The cancer is back." I was as devastated as she sounded. Even though the doctors were optimistic, she still had to go through chemotherapy again. This meant the loss of hair and tiredness for the next few months.

When Carol went through this the first time, the ordeal was instrumental in my developing a disciplined prayer and meditation regiment (See Carol's Perfection earlier in this book). And I had faith in her recovery and was persistent in letting her know. Now it was back, and I was the first person she called after talking to her husband, Wil. I felt I had let her down and I really took it personally. Had I stopped reinforcing her faith and allowed the cancer to return? I don't know.

After a few days of self doubt and unanswerable questions to God, I was able to refocus and commit to Carol's health. That week at choir practice I did the closing prayer. I told the group that we've had our few days of a pity party for Carol and that was enough. Now we were to look at Carol and see health. Visualize, pray, and expect a full recovery.

The next few weeks were much better. Carol's surgeon even told her that this was not a life threatening situation and if the chemo didn't work there were other alternatives, and not to worry. Talk about taking a sigh of relief.

Well, this was short lived. Carol developed numbness above her right eye. A CAT scan showed the cancer had metastasized to her brain. Things had gone from a bad dream to a nightmare. Now what?

This was on a Wednesday and on Thursday Carol and Wil met with the doctors to discuss treatments. Carol came to choir that night, not so much to lead us, but to be with people that loved her. Lots of people that loved her. She explained that she felt she was living in a nightmare. She had just found out that her chemo was going to be able to continue in tablet form instead of by IV, which seemed like a step forward and then this happened. Now it was radiation treatments for sure.

As I write this, the radiation treatments have ended and the radiologist is very optimistic. He expects the ten small lesions that showed up in the CAT scan to easily be handled by the radiation. If not, there are other options and this is a very treatable situation. Others in choir had known people that have gone through what Carol is experiencing and are ten years removed from it.

This time, my prayers and meditations have included getting rid of the cancer and the cancer NOT COMING BACK! Carol started the NEWSingers choir about ten years ago and we expect her to continue another ten years and beyond. Her direction and support have restored, renewed, and repaired more halos than you can imagine.

I told Carol that my experience with nightmares is that eventually you wake up and it's all over. Then you realize it was only a dream and you're OK. I, no – we expect and believe Carol's halo will be fully restored and resume its place of honor above her beautiful red hair. And we are thankful for it being so.

Music washes away
from the soul the dust of
everyday life.

- Anonymous

The friend who holds your
hand and says the wrong thing
is made of dearer stuff than the
one who stays away.

– Barbara Kingsolver

YOU'RE A LIAR

Back in the late 1950s, my friend Gail and I were listening to his sister Julie's records. We especially liked "Charlie Brown" by the Coasters. Gail's father was into electronics and Gail told me that his father talked about being able to play a record where you could turn off the music and just hear the singer, or vice versa. I can still remember looking incredulous and saying, "You're a liar." Of course, he was talking about a stereo record, but I had never heard of such a thing and figured he didn't know what he was talking about. How silly I was back then. Here I am in the 21st century and I'll believe just about any technological statement anyone makes.

Sometimes I do the same thing in my faith journey. Because I'm comfortable where I am in my faith, that I just assume others are wrong in theirs. I've seen the light and it's a shame they've chosen the wrong path. They're liars or they believe liars. How silly of me. Who am I to say anyone is wrong? Especially when I believe we are all children of the same creator. Would this creator make any of our journeys wrong? Probably not.

I, as I'm sure many have, have gone through periods of growth in my faith journey, growth that has made my previous beliefs seem childish or wrong. But they weren't wrong, they were just different than they are now. They were part of my journey to this place. So, I suppose I should allow others to travel their own road and not discourage their trek. After all, I've often been comfortable at different places along the way and would not have appreciated being called a liar when professing my faith.

Age does wonders if you let it. You can become more tolerant, more loving of all, and wiser. It's up to you. I've finally come to a place that allows me to be more respectful of another's halo no matter what condition it's in or what journey it's on. This is not always easy, but I've found it is necessary. There have been many people on my journey that have nurtured and caressed my halo to wholeness. So, if I've learned anything, it's that I can and should do the same for halos that are different than as well as the same as mine.

As my dear friend Linda has said, I need to love their halos to wholeness, whether I know what their wholeness is or not. I just need to nurture them in that direction.

I don't always understand halo repair just like I didn't understand stereo recordings. But my lack of knowledge or understanding doesn't mean it isn't so or that isn't good. And, Gail, I'm sorry I called you a liar.

What makes you think you
look better to others than they
look to you?

- Anonymous

In the faces of men and women
I see God.

- Walt Whitman

VISIT YOUR GOOD CUSTOMERS

In sales there are times when you're on a bad streak and things just aren't going your way. If you've been to as many seminars or listened to as many tapes as I have, you know that they teach you to go and visit some of your best customers when you're going through a rough spell. This is designed to remind you that there are people out there that believe in and like what you do. It's also a good time to bring them up to date on you and your company. Who knows, maybe you'll make a sale. But that's not the reason for the visit. This is a self-restorative visit. This gets you back on the horse and ready to face another day with confidence. You hear a lot of "noes" in sales, so it doesn't hurt to stop in and see a few of the "yeses."

This is also a very good idea in life. When I was divorced and living in Cleveland, I remember being very lonely. I had moved to Cleveland to get married and everyone I knew was either my former wife's relative or friends of both of us. My family and most of my friends were nearly an hour-and-a-half away. Consequently, I did quite a bit of driving during that period in my life. I really needed to be among people that loved me.

I still look for reinforcement in all that I do. I've had friends read parts of this book and asked for their feedback. It's hasn't always been positive but it's always been loving. That's what good friends and family do. And that's what I do for them. Loving, honest support is crucial to halo repair. Just make sure there's "tenderness in your honesty," as Paul Simon would say. Nurture your relationships and know who you can go to when your halo needs a jolt. Recharging your halo is a task for those who love you. Let them do it.

The best mirror is an old friend.

- George Herbert

If you have any faith, give me, for heaven's sake, a share of it! Your doubts you may keep to yourself, for I have a plenty of my own.

- Goethe

Sometimes our light goes out but is blown into flame by another human being. Each of us owes deepest thanks to those who have rekindled this light.

-Albert Schweitzer

DON'T GO CHANGING

Billy Joel had a song that was popular around the time that my wife Debbie and I were first seeing each other. "Just The Way You Are" started out with, "Don't go changing to try to please me," and Deb picked it as our song. I thought that was pretty good, because I was not unhappy with myself and I had no intention of changing. Of course, by not changing I didn't mean I would give up always trying to improve myself, but for the most part, what you see is what you get.

Now I'm not sure when it was that Deb first started to try and mold me the way she wanted me to be. It may have started right after the honeymoon. I'm not sure. It could have started during the honeymoon, but I was so drunk with sex that I don't remember. To tell the truth, I'm not sure she even spoke during the honeymoon. But that's neither here nor there. The point is it was now becoming "time to start changing to try to please me."

Now by telling this story I'm not saying that I'm not guilty of this myself. I just noticed her attempt more. Well, after some major and minor skirmishes, we've settled in to a very pleasant and fulfilling life with each other. And we pretty much love each other just the way we are.

Imagine that. Loving people just the way they are. That doesn't mean we can't help them improve or change (if they want to) or that they might not be able to help us (if we want help). It means accepting God's beloved children precisely where they are, even if we do have a few ifs, ands, or buts.

This is not an easy task. We are all guilty of knowing a better way for other people to raise their kids or treat their spouses or handle customers or live their lives. We can think of a thousand ways for others to change, but have we ever tried to change ourselves and seen how hard that can be? Try to quit smoking or swearing. Try to quit biting your nails. Try to be a safe and courteous driver and not let other drivers push your button. Try to be a more loving and responsive mate. Try to be forgiving of yourself and others. The list goes on and on and on.

If changing our own way of doing things (which, of course, is the right way) is so hard, what makes us think we can affect change in someone else? I'm not saying it's impossible, but I do believe it requires cooperation on both parts. Willingness is the beginning and help is sometimes effective.

Now back to Debbie and me. We, eventually, were able to discuss possible changes we would like to see and agreed that if we could accommodate, we would. And, through love, we've both learned to live with the things that didn't change. That's not to say we wouldn't prefer it otherwise, but it's not a relationship buster.

Accentuate the positive and recognize the other person's halo as a sign that this is God's beloved child and that God feels delight in them and is attached and devoted to them. Seeing that God is in another may not always be the easiest thing to do; however, it's the truth. And halo recognition is very important to others as well as us.

Paradise is where I am.

- Voltaire

Nothing so needs reforming as other people's habits.

- Mark Twain

SHELTERBELT

Friends of mine were going to attend a get-together held by one of their relatives in Kansas. The last of the directions indicated that they would come to a house with a shelterbelt and that would be the site. Shelterbelt was not a familiar term to them and upon arrival they discovered what it was. The house had a protective perimeter of trees around it. These trees would slow down the wind that sweeps across the Kansas plains and give the house some shelter.

Pretty smart, huh? Slowing down the weathering effect of windblown dust. This would seem to be a good idea in one's life, also. What could a person surround themselves with that would filter out the negative effects on life? If there was something, would you want to use it?

Oliver Wendell Holmes says, "If I had a formula for bypassing trouble, I would not pass it round. Trouble creates a capacity to handle it. I don't embrace trouble; that's as bad as treating it as an enemy. But I do say meet it as a friend, for you'll see a lot of it and had better be on speaking terms with it."

Imagine that, not bypassing trouble and meeting it as a friend. That's just what Jane did. When diagnosed with breast cancer in August of 1988, she decided to take charge. In her words, "I have always known inside that what we believe about things has a big impact on our life, physically and emotionally. Therefore, the day after the diagnosis, I made an appointment with a psychologist. I went for counseling because I needed to find out about the perceptions I had about myself, the cancer, and life that might be barriers to my getting well again. I had to face the fact that not only could I die from this illness, but that even without the cancer, I was still going to die someday. How could I get through this and live life as fully as possible?"

"The professional counseling taught me about my strengths. I learned that I had courage to face difficulties, such as chemotherapy, with grace, and that I had the determination to say, 'This isn't easy, but I can make myself get through it.' I also learned to draw on my personal faith, not expecting that God was going to cure me or take cancer away, but knowing that God was there to tap into for strength. The cancer experience brought me closer to my family. It showed me just how precious those relationships are and not to waste the time with those closest to me. One of the biggest lessons I learned was that although we don't have control over a lot of what happens to us, we do have power over our perceptions and our responses to what happens. We have the choice to live life fully; doing what is life-giving."

Jane went on to say "This is why I say that cancer, for me, was a gift. In many ways, my life after cancer has been far better than it was before cancer." You can read more about Jane at her website www.imagesofwellness.com.

Meeting trouble as a friend and learning to work with it instead of against it is an amazing ability. Jane's acceptance and embracing of the situation led her to the practice of imagery and relaxation techniques. As she shared this and additional information with others, she said she "connected with them in a way that really fed my soul."

Jane has accepted her gift and she has grown from it. She looked cancer in the eye and said, "Hi!" Her halo now shines with a new purpose and meaning. It's no longer "Why me?" It's, "What will I do now? How will I take this situation and turn it into an opportunity for healing and personal growth?" No shelterbelt for her. Jane just accepts life as it comes. What a wonderful life she has. And she and her halo really appreciate it.

Laughter is inner jogging.

- Norman Cousins

If we are not responsible for
the thoughts that pass our
doors, we are at least
responsible for those we admit
and entertain.

- Charles B. Newcomb

KNOCK AND THE DOOR WILL OPEN

Ask – it'll be given to you; seek – you'll find; knock – it'll be opened for you.

In my life this has been one of the most intriguing things that Jesus ever said. As a young boy, I was often disappointed to find out that this wasn't working like I thought it should. Even into adulthood, my asking, seeking, and knocking seemed not to give, find, or open the goody bag I wanted. It wasn't until my late thirties and early forties that I began to comprehend this wonderful verse.

Asking, seeking, and knocking were not to be taken lightly. The passing whimsy of a red bicycle or a transistor radio or a yellow Mustang doesn't fit. When dealing with powers of this magnitude, there must be passion and commitment. There must be belief and love. There must be joy and kindness. God loves you and will honor your beliefs.

So, I make the effort to honor God in all I do, think, and say. And God has blessed me with an amazing life full of family, friends, love, and abundance. And you know what? I keep asking for more and I get it. I seek new ways of expressing myself and I find them. I knock and doors open for me. I expect and look for good and I find it everywhere. I love life and life loves me. I give to life and life gives to me. What a wonderful relationship.

The hymn writer, Civila Martin, said it perfectly, "I sing because I'm happy. I sing because I'm free. God's eye is on the sparrow. And I know God watches me." And my halo.

The words "I am…" are potent words; be careful what you hitch them to. The thing you're claiming has a way of reaching back and claiming you.

- A.L. Kitselman

Happiness comes when your work and words are of benefit to yourself and others.

- Buddha

The best remedy for those who are afraid, lonely or unhappy is to go outside, somewhere where they can be quiet, alone with the heavens, nature and God. Because only then does one feel that all is as it should be and that God wishes to see people happy, amidst the simple beauty of nature.

- Anne Frank

AUSTIN'S ANGEL

It was bedtime and three-year old Austin wouldn't go to bed. He and his parents lived in a small apartment over a dry cleaners and Austin was, usually, pretty good about bedtime. This was because he had an angel that he played with, and he and his angel had no problem going to his room when it was time to go to sleep. However, this night he was crying that he didn't want to go to bed. His mother said to just take his angel with him and everything would be all right. Through his tears, Austin said that she flew away through the window and he didn't want to go to his room.

His mom calmed him down and he fell asleep on the couch while they were watching TV. When his parents went to bed, they put a blanket over him and let him sleep on the couch. Later that night they were awakened by smoke. An electrical fire had started in Austin's bedroom. His dad scooped him up and the three of them ran out of the apartment. The fire department put out the blaze after significant damage was done to the apartment and the business below. Austin's angel was back playing with him the next day.

I get goose bumps every time I tell this story. A three-year-old with an angel for a playmate. And I've yet to tell it to someone that didn't believe it.

This is the kind of tale that warms your heart and strengthens your faith. The innocence of a young child's casual acceptance of God's love in the form of an angel playmate is a powerful lesson to the rest of us. We often look so hard for God's presence that we can't see the angels for the humanity that we're surrounded by.

HALO REPAIR

My wife Debbie, who went to Catholic school, said that in first and second grade the nuns would tell them to slide over and make room for their guardian angels to sit next to them. Then from third grade on, there was no mention of guardian angels, and she wondered why. Was it time to start setting aside childish things?

God's precious angels are everywhere. Let those who have eyes see. See an angel in your lover. See angels in children. See angels in friends. See them in coworkers. See them in everyone you come in contact with. I know this can be hard, but God *is* in everyone. And if that doesn't make you an angel, I don't know what does. Many people don't even know this or believe it. That's why you need to see the angel in them for them.

Help reveal another's halo and yours will be revealed to them. They may not realize it at the time, but after awhile it may start to sink in. Then they'll find out what Austin already knows – that angels are loving, playful creatures who truly care about you.

Friends are angels who lift us
to our feet when our wings
have trouble remembering how
to fly.

- Anonymous

Angels say "halo" to everyone.

- Anonymous

OUTSIDE THE VASE

As we sat there discussing the different ways God can be worshipped, we were directed to look at the beautiful display that had been set up. To help set the mood, Debbie Page, one of the facilitators, had placed on the table a striking arrangement using four separate fabrics, several votive candles, praying hands, an angel picture, and a cross. We were asked to pick something from the table that stood out to us and explain why we thought it caught our attention.

One of the votive candles had been placed in a transparent red glass vase. This is what caught my eye. The vase just glowed with flickering light from the candle. Others in the group were talking while I continued to stare at the candle in the vase. After a moment of silence, I spoke. To me the candle represented me, letting my light shine. And the vase represented the spirit of God. The idea being that, instead of just being a light in the world, I should let my light shine through God's spirit. This not only is light-enhancing but it softened the glare of just a bare candle.

Sometimes I just let my light shine without God's loving and light-enhancing filter. And it can be a little harsh and hard to take. So I try to be more purposeful in my exposure to the world and present myself as a candle in a vase. It is an effort that I'm hoping will become a habit. I've often found myself in situations where I've caught myself outside the vase and had to take a moment to get to where I needed to be. And other times, I didn't realize I was outside the vase until it was too late. These are called learning experiences, if I learn from them.

After the class, I realized that it goes the other way, too. We can look at another person's light and not see it "in the vase" – not see it wrapped in the God-spirit. What if we automatically put everyone's light in the vase, whether they put themselves there or not? Would that make a difference in how we received their light? I believe it would. In all our encounters, we place the other person's light in the vase. Envelop it in the spirit of God. See them in the light of love.

One other thing I noticed about a candle in a vase is that when the flame shines through the glass it has a little halo around it. Imagine that! If you wrap your light in the God-spirit a halo appears. Sounds like an idea for a book.

In the right light,

at the right time,

everything is extraordinary.

\- Aaron Rose

There are two kinds of light,
the glow that illuminates
and the glare that obscures.

- James Thurber

ORDERING INFORMATION

FOR

HALO REPAIR

A Nudge Toward Wholeness

By
Bill Fiest

To place book orders, go to www.HaloRepair.com

If you would like to purchase
"And a voice came from Heaven" cards
or "Pretty Lady" prints,
go to www.HaloRepair.com

If you're interested in workshops
or speaking engagements,
go to www.HaloRepair.com
for more information
as it becomes available.

Live as you want to be
remembered.

- Anonymous